The School Garden

by **Anne Giulieri**

illustrated by Garry Fleming

This is the water tank
at my school.

The rain comes down.
It goes into the tank.

This is the school garden.

The water in the tank goes on the garden.

Carrots are in the garden.

We cannot see the carrots.

They are hiding!

Peas are in the garden.

We cannot see the peas.

They are hiding!

peas

Tomatoes are in the garden.

We cannot see the tomatoes.

They are hiding, too!

The water in the tank
goes on the garden.

Look in the garden!

A little carrot is coming.

Carrots

Look in the garden!
A little pea is coming.

Look in the garden!

A little tomato is coming.

We can see carrots.
We can see peas.
We can see tomatoes.

They are good to eat!